I WAS THE WIND LAST NIGHT

Also by Ruskin Bond in Speaking Tiger

Lone Fox Dancing: My Autobiography
A Book of Simple Living: Brief Notes from the Hills
Friends in Wild Places: Birds, Beasts and Other Companions
A Little Book of Happiness
A Little Book of Serenity
A Little Book of Love and Companionship

Edited Volumes
Himalaya: Adventure, Meditation, Life (with Namita Gokhale)
Prankenstein: A Book of Crazy Mischief (with Jerry Pinto)

I WAS THE *Wind Last Night*

New and Collected
POEMS

RUSKIN BOND

SPEAKING
TIGER

SPEAKING TIGER PUBLISHING PVT. LTD
4381/4 Ansari Road, Daryaganj,
New Delhi–110002, India

First published in hardback by Speaking Tiger 2017

Copyright © Ruskin Bond 2017

ISBN: 978-93-87164-14-7
eISBN: 978-93-87164-12-3

10 9 8 7 6 5 4 3 2 1

The moral right of the author has been asserted.

Typeset in Goudy Old Style by Jojy Philip
Printed at

All rights reserved.

No part of this publication may be reproduced,
transmitted, or stored in a retrieval system, in any form or
by any means, electronic, mechanical, photocopying,
recording or otherwise, without the prior
permission of the publisher.

This book is sold subject to the condition that it shall not,
by way of trade or otherwise, be lent, resold, hired out,
or otherwise circulated, without the publisher's
prior consent, in any form of binding or cover
other than that in which it is published.

Somehow I've got through life
With just a modicum of strife;
I've bumbled along,
Humming my song,
And if I'm born again,
I'd happily be
A humble hummable bumblebee!

—RB

Contents

Author's Note   xi

A Peepul Tree I Knew
I Roam No More	3
The Trees	4
Flowers I Have Known	5
Commelina	7
Raindrop	8
On Wings of Sleep	9
Garhwal Himalaya	10
Parts of Old Dehra	11
Pebbles	13
The Small Red Ant	14
Trees of God	15
Banyan Tree	16
The Fern	17
The Snail	18
Look for the Colours of Life	19
A Little Night Music	21
Rain	23
So Beautiful the Night	24
A Frog Screams	25

Silent Birth	26
Cherry Tree	27
The Owl	29
Tigers Forever	30
The Snake	31
Once You Have Lived with Mountains	32
Butterfly Time	33
The Whistling Schoolboy	34
Dandelion	35
A Bedbug Gives Thanks	37
Walnut Tree	38
To the Indian Foresters	39
This Land Is Mine	40

Remember the Old Road

The Pool	43
Remember the Old Road	44
Come Roaming With Me	46
Spell Broken	47
Hill Station	48
Lost	49
Walnut Tree Revisited	51
Return to Dehra	52
Survivor's Song	53

Friends, Far and Near

Kites	57
A Song for Lost Friends	59

Going Home	74
I Was the Wind Last Night	75
Lullaby	76
Summer Fruit	77
Granny's Tree-climbing	78
What Can We Give Our Children	80
Don't Be Afraid of the Dark	81
View From the Window	82
Boy in a Blue Pullover	83
To Live in Magic	84
October	85
Granny's Proverbs	87
We Rode All the Way to Delhi	88
My Best Friend	90

We Must Keep Loving, All Our Days

It Isn't Time That's Passing	93
Love Lyrics for Binya Devi	94
The Love of Two Stars	98
Lovers Observed	99
Phantom Lover	100
We Must Keep Loving, All Our Days	101
Primrose Hill	102
Passing By	103
Love's Sad Song	104
Love Is a Law	105
One Flower	106

I'll Take the Road Alone

Listen!	109
Rain in the Hills	110
Night Thoughts	111
Out of the Darkness	112
Wild Is the Wind	113
A Quiet Mind	114
Lone Fox Dancing	115
The Bat	116
Firefly in My Room	117
For Silence	118
In This Workaday World	119

If Mice Could Roar

Evening by the Fireside	123
Cricket-Field Placings	124
A Plea for Bowlers	125
Foot Soldiers	126
Song for a Beetle	127
The Cat Has Something to Say	129
A Nightmare	130
Hip-Hop Nature Boy	131
In Praise of the Sausage	134
If Mice Could Roar	135
Night Rhyme	136
The Demon Driver	137
Do You Believe in Ghosts?	139
In a Strange Cafe	140
And So to Bed	142

The Silent Stones

The Good For Nothing	145
September Morn	146
Who'll Buy My Poems?	147
Secondhand Shop in Hill Station	148
Lost All My Money	150
We Are the Babus	151
Slum Children at Play	152
Home from the Burning-Ghat	154
Dragonflies	155
Midwinter, Deserted Hill Station	156
Song of the Cockroach	157

Odds and Ends

Self Portrait	161
Haikus	162
Portents	165
Good Omens, Good Companions	166
Consolations	167
To Light a Fire	169
Night in the Mountains: Garhwal	170
Nights in the Hills: Landour	171
Out of the Dark	172

And As We Part

All Is Life	177
At the Grave of John Mildenhall in Agra	178
Last Words	180
Hold on to Your Dreams	181

Dare to Dream	182
We Who Love Books	183
These Simple Things	184
And As We Part	185
About the Author	186

Author's Note

I did not write much poetry until I came to live in the hills. Some of these poems were written at Maplewood Lodge, Mussoorie in the 1960s and '70s. Others, at Ivy Cottage, Landour, from 1980 to the present.

—R.B.

A Peepul tree
I KNEW

I Roam No More

I roam no more.
But I can still
See conifers upon this hill
And hear the pines
Whisper in the dark,
Talking to themselves;
For the earth is theirs by right.
And we are but trespassers
By day,
And aliens
In the night.

The Trees

At seven, when dusk slips over the mountains,
The trees start whispering among themselves.
They have been standing still all day,
But now they stretch their limbs in the dark,
Shifting a little, flexing their fingers,
Remembering the time when
They too walked the earth with men.
They know me well, these trees:
Oak and walnut, spruce and pine,
They know my face in the window,
They know me for a dreamer of dreams,
A world-loser, one of them.
They watch me while I watch them grow.
I listen to their whisperings,
Their own mysterious diction;
And bow my head before their arms
And ask for benediction.

Flowers I Have Known

1

Lovely have been the flowers
That kept me company
These many years
Of lonely walks and solitude.
Now, upon an old wall
I lean, a dandelion for company,
Recalling flowers I have known:
The iris, like a prayer-flag on the hill,
Wild roses near a mountain stream,
A crowd of sunflowers
Turning with the sun,
And violets—
Violets springing a surprise
In early Spring,
When flowers are rare.
But all the year
The ferns are here,
They raise
Their fronds
In shaded corners
Free from frost.

2

In Winter dreams
Himalayan poppies bend
To the bracing wind,
And rhododendrons fling
Red petals at my feet.

Commelina

Concealed among a tangle
Of hart's-tongue fern,
Your brilliant blue
Recognizing me for an instant,
For I have been here before—
Long ago, when I was young
And Binya took me by the hand
And pointed you out to me.
I haven't seen her for many years,
But you are still here, commelina,
Springing up every year,
Constant among the ferns.

Raindrop

This leaf, so complete in itself,
Is only part of a tree.
And this tree, so complete in itself,
Is only part of the mountain.
And the mountain runs down to the sea.
And the sea, so complete in itself,
Rests like a raindrop
On the hand of God.

On Wings of Sleep

On wings of sleep
I dreamt I flew
Across the valley drenched in dew
Over the roof-tops
Into the forest
Swooping low
Where the Sambhur belled
And the peacocks flew.
And the dawn broke
Rose-pink behind the mountains
And the river ran silver and gold
As I glided over the trees
Drifting with the dawn breeze
Across the river,
Over fields of corn.
And the world awoke
To a new day, a new dawn.
Time to fly home,
As the sun rose, red and angry,
Ready to singe my wings,
I returned to my sleeping form,
Creaking bed and dusty window-pane,
To dream of flying with the wind again.

Garhwal Himalaya

Deep in the crouching mist, lie the mountains.
Climbing the mountains are forests
Of rhododendron, spruce and deodar—
Trees of God, we call them—soughing
In the wind from the passes of Garhwal;
And the snow-leopard moans softly
When the herdsmen pass, their lean sheep cropping
Short winter grass.
And clinging to the sides of the mountains,
The small stone houses of Garhwal,
Their thin fields of calcinated soil torn
From the old spirit-haunted rocks.
Pale women plough, they laugh at the thunder,
As their men go down to the plains:
Little grows on the beautiful mountains
In the east wind.
There is hunger of children at noon; and yet
There are those who sing of the sunset
And the gods and glories of Himaal,
Forgetting no one eats sunsets.
Wonder, then, at the absence of old men;
For some grow old at their mothers' breasts,
In cold Garhwal.

Written at Chamba, 1960.

Parts of Old Dehra

Parts of old Dehra remain…
A peepul tree I knew
And flying foxes
In a mango grove
And here and there
A moss-encrusted wall
Old bungalows
Gone to seed
And giving way
To concrete slabs.
A garden town's become a city
And the people faceless
As they pass or rather rush
Hell-bent
From place of work
To crowded tenement.
So change must come,
Fields make way for factories,
The trees succumb
To real-estate,
The rivers plunge
Silt-laden

To our doom.
Too late to do a thing
About it now,
For we have grown
Too many,
And the world's no bigger
Than before.
Do-gooders, don't despair!
Nature will repair
Her own, long after
We are dust.

Pebbles

Pebbles on the seashore.
Millions of pebbles, and yet each one is different.
I pick up a pebble and throw it far out to sea.
For thousands of years the sea will roll over it,
And the pebble will become smoother and
    rounder,
But after all that time it will still be a pebble,
As you made it, as I threw it.
After all, what is a thousand years?

The Small Red Ant

You stride through the wasteland of my desk,
Pressing on over books and papers,
Down the wall and across the floor—
Small red ant, now crossing a sea of raindrops
At my open door.
Your destiny, your task
To carry home
That heavy sunflower seed,
Waving it like a banner
Of victory!

*

And you stride through the long grass,
Pressing on over fallen pine needles,
Up the winding road to the mountain pass:
Small red ant, now crossing a sea
Of snow; your destiny
To carry home that single, slender
Cosmos seed,
Waving it like a banner in the sun.

Trees of God

Trees of God, we call them;
Planted here when the world was young,
The first trees
Their fingers pointing to the stars,
Older than the cedars of Lebanon.

They cut them down last spring
With swift efficient tools,
The sap was rising still.
The trees bled,
Slaughtered
To make furniture for fools.

Banyan Tree

I remember you well, old banyan tree
As you stood there, spreading quietly
Over the broken wall.
While adults slept, I crept away
Down the broad veranda steps, around
The outhouse and the melon-ground
Into the shades of afternoon.
Those summers in India no one stirred
Till evening brought the Fever-Bird
And the mem-sahibs rose with the Rising Moon.
In that June of long ago, I roamed
The faded garden of my father's home;
He'd gone away. There was nothing to do
And no one to talk to….
I must have known that giants have few friends
(The great lurk shyly in their private dens)—
And found you hidden by a dark green wall
Of aerial roots.
Intruder in your pillared den, I stood
And shyly touched your old and rugged wood.
And as my hands explored you, giant tree,
I heard you singing!

The Fern

The slender maidenhair fern grows firm on a rock,
While all around her the water swirls and chatters
And then disappears in a rush
Down to the bottom of the hill.
When I'm surrounded by troubled waters, Lord,
Let me find within a rock to cling to,
And give me the quiet patience of the maidenhair
Who has learned to live with the rock.

The Snail

Leaving the safety of a rocky ledge
The snail sets out
On his long journey
Across a busy path.
The grass is greener on the other side!
For tender leaf or juicy stem
He'll brave the hazards of the road.
Not made to dodge or weave or run,
He must await each threatening step
Chancing his luck.
Keeping his tentacles crossed!
Though all unaware
Of the dangers of being squashed,
He does not pause or flinch—
A cartwheel misses by an inch!—
But slithers on.
Intent on dinner.
He's there at last, his prize—
Rich leaf-mould where the grass grows tall.
I salute you, Snail.
Somehow, you've made me feel quite small.

Look for the Colours of Life

Colours are everywhere,
Bright blue the sky,
Dark green the forest
And light the fresh grass,
Bright yellow the lights
From a train sweeping past,
The Flame trees glow
At this time of year,
The mangoes burn bright
As the monsoon draws near.

A favourite colour of mine
Is the pink of the candyfloss man
As he comes down the dusty road,
Calling his wares,
And the balloon-man soon follows,
Selling his floating bright colours.
It's early summer
And the roses blush
In the dew-drenched dawn,
And poppies sway red and white
In the invisible breeze.
Only the wind has no colour:

But if you look carefully
You will see it teasing
The colour out of the leaves.
And the rain has no colour
But it turns the bronzed grass
To emerald green,
And gives a golden sheen
To the drenched sunflower.
Look for the colours of life—
They are everywhere,
Even in your dreams.

A Little Night Music

Open the window
Let in the Night
All that is lovely
Comes at this hour
Moonlight and moonbeam
And fragrance of flower
Blossoming Champa
And Queen of the Night—
And sometimes a field mouse
Drops in for a bite.
High in the treetops
An owl strikes a note
And the frogs in their pond
Sing out as they float
Along on their lily pads…
The brainfever bird
Is calling on high
'Brain fever, brain fever!'—
Its monotonous cry.
The nightjar plays trombone
The crickets join in
An out-of-tune orchestra
Making a din!
I lie awake listening

To the wild duck in flight
As they fly to the north
For their annual respite;
And a star in the heavens
Sweeps past as it falls,
A leopard's out hunting—
The swamp deer calls.
A breeze has sprung up,
It hums in the trees
The window is rattling
And I must cease
From my Nocturne
And shut out the Night.
Goodnight, birds
Goodnight, frogs
Goodnight, stars
Goodnight sweet Night.

Rain

After weeks of heat and dust
How welcome is the rain.
It washes the leaves,
Gives new life to grass,
Draws out the scent of the earth.
It rattles on the roof,
Gurgles along the drainpipe
Collects in a puddle in the middle of the lawn—
The birds come to bathe.

When the sun comes out
A lizard crawls up from a crack in a rock.
'Small brown lizard
Basking in the sun
You too have your life to live
Your race to run.'
At night we look through the branches
Of the cherry tree.
The sky is rainwashed, star-bright.

So Beautiful the Night

I love the night, Lord.
After the sun's heat and the day's work,
It's good to close my eyes and rest my body.
It's a good time for small creatures:
Porcupines come out of their burrows to dig for roots.
The nightjar calls tonk-tonk!
The timid owl peeps out of his hole in the tree trunk
Where he has been hiding all day.
Insects crawl out in thousands.
The wind comes down the chimney and blows around the room.
I'm watching the stars from my window.
The trees are stretching their arms in the dark and whispering to the moon.
But if the trees could walk, Lord,
What a wonderful sight it would be—
Armies of pines and firs and oaks
Marching over the moonlit mountains.

A Frog Screams

Standing near a mountain stream
I heard a sound like the creaking
Of a branch in the wind.
It was a frog screaming
In the jaws of a long green snake.

I couldn't bear that hideous cry.
And taking two sharp sticks,
I made the twisting snake disgorge the frog,
Who hopped quite spry out of the snake's mouth
And sailed away on a floating log.

Pleased with the outcome,
I released the green grass-snake,
Stood back and spoke aloud:
'Is this what it feels like to be God?'
'Only what it's like to be English,'
Said God (speaking for a change in French);
'I would have let the snake finish his lunch!'

Silent Birth

When the earth gave birth to this tree,
There came no sound:
A green shoot thrust
In silence from the ground.
Our births don't come so quiet—
Most lives run riot—
But the bud opens silently,
And flower gives way to fruit.
So must we search
For the stillness within the tree,
The silence within the root.

Cherry Tree

Eight years have passed
Since I placed my cherry seed in the grass.
'Must have a tree of my own,' I said—
And watered it once and went to bed
And forgot; but cherries have a way of growing
Though no one's caring very much or knowing,
And suddenly that summer, near the end of May,
I found a tree had come to stay.
It was very small, a five months' child,
Lost in the tall grass running wild.
Goats ate the leaves, a grasscutter's scythe
Split it apart, and a monsoon blight
Shrivelled the slender stem... Even so,
Next spring I watched three new shoots grow,
The young tree struggle, upwards thrust
Its arms in a fresh fierce lust
For light and air and sun.
I could only wait, as one
Who watches, wondering, while Time and the rain
Made a miracle from green, growing pain...

I went away next year—
Spent a season in Kashmir—
Came back thinner, rather poor,
But richer by a cherry tree at my door.
Six feet high, my own dark cherry,
And—I could scarcely believe it—a berry,
Ripened and jewelled in the sun,
Hung from a branch—just one!
And next year there were blossoms, small
Pink, fragile, quick to fall
At the merest breath, the sleepiest breeze…

I lay on the grass, at ease,
Looked up through leaves, at the blue
Blind sky, at the finches as they flew
And flitted through the dappled green,
While bees in an ecstasy drank
Of nectar from each bloom, and the sun sank
Swiftly, and the stars turned in the sky,
And moon-moths and singing crickets and I—
Yes, I!—praised night and stars and tree:
A small, tall cherry grown by me.

The Owl

At night, when all is still,
The forest's sentinel
Glides silently across the hill
And perches in an old pine tree.
A friendly presence his!
No harm can come
From night bird on the prowl.
His cry is mellow,
Much softer than a peacock's call.
Why then this fear of owls
Calling in the night?
If men must speak,
Then owls must hoot—
They have the right.
On me it casts no spell:
Rather, it seems to cry,
'The night is good—all's well, all's well.'

Tigers Forever

May there always be tigers, Lord.
In the jungles and tall grass
May the tiger's roar be heard,
May his thunder
Be known in the land.
At the forest pool, by moonlight
May he drink and raise his head
Scenting the night wind.
May he crouch low in the grass
When the herdsmen pass,
And slumber in dark caverns
When the sun is high.
May there always be tigers, Lord.
But not so many that one of them
Might be tempted to come into my bedroom
In search of a meal!

The Snake

When, after days of rain,
The sun appears
The snake emerges,
Green-gold on the grass.
Kept in so long,
He basks for hours
Soaks up the hot bright sun.
Knowing how shy he is of me,
I walk a gentle pace
Letting him doze in peace.
But to the snake, earth-bound,
Each step must sound like thunder.
He glides away,
Goes underground.
I've known him for some years:
A harmless green grass-snake
Who, when he sees me on the path,
Uncoils and disappears.

Once You Have Lived with Mountains

Once you have lived with mountains
Under the whispering pines
And deodars, near stars
And a brighter moon,
With wood smoke and mist
Sweet smell of grass, dew lines
On spider-spun, sun-kissed
Buttercup and vine;
Once you have lived with these,
Blessed, God's favourite then,
You will return,
You will come back
To touch the trees and grass
And climb once more the windswept
    mountain pass.

Butterfly Time

April showers
Bring swarms of butterflies
Streaming across the valley
Seeking sweet nectar.
Yellow, gold, and burning bright,
Red and blue and banded white.
To my eyes they bring delight!
Theirs a long and arduous flight,
Here today and off tomorrow,
Floating on, bright butterflies,
To distant bowers.
For Nature does things in good order:
And birds and butterflies recognize
No man-made border.

The Whistling Schoolboy

From the gorge above Gangotri
Down to Kochi by the sea,
The whistling-thrush keeps singing
That same sweet melody.

He was a whistling schoolboy once,
Who heard god Krishna's flute,
And tried to play the same sweet tune,
But touched a faulty note.

Said Krishna to the errant youth—
A bird you must become,
And you shall whistle all your days
Until your song is done.

Dandelion

I think it's an insult
To Nature's generosity
That many call this cheerful flower
A 'common weed'.
How dare they so degrade
A flower divinely made!
Sublimely does it bloom and seed
In sunshine or in shade,
Thriving in wind and rain,
On stony soil
On walls or steps
On strips of waste;
Tough and resilient,
Giving delight
When other flowers are out of sight.

And when its puff-ball comes to fruit
You make a wish and blow it clean away
'Please make my wish come true,' you say.
And if you're kind and pure of heart,
Who knows? This magic flower might
    just respond

And help you on your way.
Good dandelion,
Be mine today!

A Bedbug Gives Thanks

I'm a child of the Universe
Claimed the bug
As he crawled out of the woodwork.
I've every right
To be a blight.
To Infinite Intelligence I owe
My place—
Chief pest
Upon the human race!
I'm here to stay—
To feast upon their delicate display,
Those luscious thighs,
Those nooks and crannies
Where the blood runs sweet.
No, no, I don't despise
These creatures made for my delight.
A kind Creator had my needs in mind;
I thank you, Lord, for human-kind.

Walnut Tree

The walnut tree is the first to lose its leaves,
But at the same time the fruit ripens,
The skin splits, the hard shell of the nut
Stands revealed. Yesterday (the last of August)
You climbed among the last few crumpled leaves,
Slim boy in a walnut tree, your toes
Gripping the tender bark, your fingers
Fondling walnuts, while I waited and counted,
And there were twenty-three walnuts on the grass.
We cracked them open with our teeth.
They were still raw but we could not wait:
The walnuts would age and I might grow younger!

To the Indian Foresters

You are the quiet men who do not boast
Although you've done much more than most
To make this land a sea of green
From here to far Cape Comorin.
Without your help to Nature's thrust,
This land would be a bowl of dust.
A land without its forest wealth
Must suffer a decline in health,
For herbs and plants all need green cover
Before they help the sick recover.
And we need trees to hold together
Beasts, and birds of every feather,
And leaves to help the air smell sweet;
And this and more is no mean feat.
Dear foresters, you have not sought for fame or
    favour,
Yours has been a love of labour.
Our thanks! Instead of desert sand
You've given us this green and growing land.

(Composed and read to a gathering of young forest officers at the Forest Research Institute on 10 April 2004)

This Land Is Mine

This land is mine
Although I do not own it,
This land is mine
Because I grew upon it.
This dust, this grass,
This tender leaf
And weathered bark
All in my heart are finely blended
Until my time on earth is ended.

REMEMBER THE Old Road

The Pool

Where has it gone,
> the pool on the hill?
The pool of our youth,
> when Time stood still,
Where we romped in its shallows
> and wrestled on sand,
Closer than brothers, a colourful band.

Gone is the pool, now filled in with rocks,
Having made way for the builders' blocks.
But sometimes, at dawn,
> you will hear us still,
And that's why they call this
> the Haunted Hill.

Remember the Old Road

Remember the old road,
The steep stony path
That took us up from Rajpur,
Toiling and sweating
And grumbling at the climb,
But enjoying it all the same.
At first the hills were hot and bare,
But then there were trees near Jharipani
And we stopped at the Halfway House
And swallowed lungfuls of diamond-cut air.
Then onwards, upwards, to the town,
Our appetites to repair!

Well, no one uses the old road any more.
Walking is out of fashion now.
And if you have a car to take you
Swiftly up the motor-road
Why bother to toil up a disused path?
You'd have to be an old romantic like me
To want to take that route again.
But I did it last year,
Pausing and plodding and gasping for air—

Both road and I being a little worse for wear!
But I made it to the top and stopped to rest
And looked down to the valley and the silver stream
Winding its way towards the plains.
And the land stretched out before me, and the years fell away,
And I was a boy again,
And the friends of my youth were there beside me,
And nothing had changed.

Come Roaming With Me

Out of the city and over the hill,
Into the spaces where Time stands still,
Under the tall trees, touching old wood,
Taking the way where warriors once stood;
Crossing the little bridge, losing my way,
But finding a friendly place where I can stay.
Those were the days, friend, when we were strong
And strode down the road to an old marching song
When the dew on the grass was fresh every morn,
And we woke to the call of the ring-dove at dawn.
The years have gone by, and sometimes I falter,
But still I set out for a stroll or a saunter,
For the wind is as fresh as it was in my youth,
And the peach and the pear still the sweetest
    of fruit,
So cast away care and come roaming with me,
Where the grass is still green and the air is
    still free.

Spell Broken

We crouched before the singing fire
As the green wood writhed and bled
And the orange flames leapt higher
And your cheeks in the dark glowed red.
Alone in the forest, you and I; and then,
Came an old gypsy to warm his feet,
And shouting children, and two young men,
And pots and pans and a hunk of meat,
And a woman who shivered and sang to herself,
And a dog of enormous size!

You were laughing and singing an old love song,
Sweet as the whistling-thrush at dawn.
Swift as the running days of November,
Lost like a dream too brief to remember.

Hill-Station

There is nothing to keep me here,
Only these mountains of silence
And the gentle reserve of shepherds and woodmen
Who know me as one who
Walks among trees.

Madman, misanthropist? They make
Their guesses, smile and pass slowly
Down the steep path near the cottage. There is
    nothing
To keep me here, walking
Among old trees.

Lost

I boarded the big ship bound for the West,
The clean white liner.
In the noon-day heat
Coolies thronged the sun-drenched pier.
Yet I saw only
The village I had left,
And a boat at rest
On the river's shallow water
In the shade of the flowering
Long red-fingered poinsettia.
I saw not the big waves
But the ripple of running
Water in the reeds.

We came to London, lost in November mist:
In an ash-grey dawn at Tilbury dock
I longed for the warmth of a kiss
Of sunlight.

In the busy streets
Were cavalcades of people

Hurrying in a heat of hope.
But I saw only

The wheat-field, the tea-slope…
A cow at rest.
And longed for the soft, shoeless tread
Of a village boy…

Walnut Tree Revisited

You have ripened, since last the walnut tree
Lost its dark leaves, last autumn.
One summer intervened between your growing
And my importunity;
One summer lost, while walnuts grew;
I too had forgotten.

We saw each other often,
But gone was the magic
Of that first encounter;
And even the tree
Gave little fruit last year.
Now it stands bare-branched
Outside the closed window,
Touched no more by feet and questing fingers,
But turning its own fingers
To the slanting winter sun.
Not one leaf left, where hundreds
Glittered like spears in the forest of September.

But I will wait until the parrots bring
Shrill portents of another spring;
(And I will love you with the same sweet pain,
If you and summer care to visit me again.)

Return to Dehra

This is old Dehra
Of mangoes and lemons
Where I grew up
Beside the jacaranda
Planted by my father
On the sunny side
Of the long veranda.
This is the house
Since sold
To Major General Mehra.
The town has grown,
None knows me now
Who knew
My mother's laughter.
Most men come home as strangers.
And yet,
The trees my father planted here—
These spreading trees—
Are still at home in Dehra.

Survivor's Song

When I was ten, I was lonely and read books.
At fifteen, I played football with other boys.
When I was twenty, I courted the girls.
At thirty, I thought time had passed too swiftly.
When I was forty, I concluded that I was a failure.
But at fifty, as I was still alive and well, I knew I
    was a success.
At sixty, I played old music and fell in love again.
At seventy, I went in search of old friends.
And at eighty, I found they had all gone away.

Kites

Are you listening to me, boy?
I am only your kitemaker,
My poems are flimsy things
Torn by the wind, caught in mango trees,
Gay sport for boys and dreamers.
My silent songs. But once I fashioned
A kite like a violin,
She sang most mournfully, like the wind
In tall deodars.

Are you listening? Remember
The Dragon Kite I made one summer?
No, you are too young. A great
Kite, with small mirrors to catch the sun
And eyes and a tongue, and gold
Trappings and a trailing silver tail.
A kite for the gods to ride!
And it rose most sweetly, but the wind
Came up from nowhere,

A wind in waiting for us,
My twine snapped and the wind took the kite,

Took it over the flat roofs
And the waving trees and the river
And the blue hills for ever.
No one knew where it fell. Boy, are you
Listening? All my kites
Are torn, but for you I'll make a bright
New poem to fly.

A Song for Lost Friends

The past is always with us, for it feeds
    the present...

1

As a boy I stood on the edge of the
    railway-cutting,
Outside the dark tunnel, my hands touching
The hot rails, waiting for them to tremble
At the coming of the noonday train.
The whistle of the engine hung on the
    forest's silence.
Then out of the tunnel, a green-gold dragon
Came plunging, thundering past—
Out of the tunnel, out of the grinning dark.

And the train rolled on, every day
Hundreds of people coming or going or
    running away—
Goodbye, goodbye!
I haven't seen you again, bright boy at the
    carriage window,
Waving to me, calling,

But I've loved you all these years and looked for
    you everywhere,
In cities and villages, beside the sea,
In the mountains, in crowds at distant places;

Returning always to the forest's silence,
To watch the windows of some passing train…

2

My father took me by the hand and led me
Among the ruins of old forts and palaces.
We lived in a tent near the tomb of Humayun,
Among old trees. Now multi-storeyed blocks
Rise from the plain—tomorrow's ruins…
You can explore them, my son, when the trees
Take over again and the thorn-apple grows
In empty windows. There were seven cities
    before…

Nothing my father said could bring my
    mother home;
She had gone with another. He took me to
    the hills
In a small train, the engine having palpitations
As it toiled up the steep slopes peopled
With pines and rhododendrons. Through tunnels
To Simla. Boarding school. He came to see me
In the holidays. We caught butterflies together.

'Next year,' he said, 'when the War is over,
We'll go to England.' But wars are never over
And I have yet to go to England with my father.

He died that year
And I was dispatched to my mother and
    stepfather—
A long journey through a dark tunnel.
No one met me at the station. So I wandered
Round Dehra in a tonga, looking for a house
With lichi trees. She'd written to say there were
    lichis in the garden.
But in Dehra all the houses had lichi trees,
The tonga-driver charged five rupees for taking
    me back to the station.
They were looking for me on the platform:
'We thought the train would be late as usual.'
It had arrived on time, upsetting everyone's
    schedule.

In my new home I found a new baby in a
    new pram.
Your little brother, they said; which made me
    a hundred.
But he too was left behind with the servants
When my mother and Mr H. went hunting
Or danced late at the casino, our only
    wartime nightclub.

Tommies and Yanks scuffled drunk and disorderly
In a private war for the favours of stale women.

Lonely in the house with the servants and the child
And books I'd read twice and my father's letters,
Treasured secretly in the small trunk beneath
    my bed:
I wrote to him once but did not post the letter,
For fear it might come back 'Return to sender...'

One day I slipped into the guava orchard
    next door—
It really belonged to Seth Hari Kishore
Who'd gone to the Ganga on a pilgrimage—
The guavas were ripe and ready for boys to steal
(Always sweeter when stolen)
And a bare leg thrust at me as I climbed:

'There's only room for one,' came a voice.
I looked up at a boy who had blackberry eyes
And guava juice on his chin, grabbed at him
And we both tumbled out of the tree
On to the ragged December grass. We rolled
    and fought
But not for long. A gardener came shouting,
And we broke and ran—over the gate and down
    the road
And across the fields and a dry river bed,

Into the shades of afternoon…
'Why didn't you run home?' he said.
'Why didn't you?'
'There's no one there, my mother's out.'
'And mine's at home.'

3

His mother was Burmese; his father
An English soldier killed in the War.
They were waiting for it to be over.
Every day, beyond the gardens, we loafed:
Time was suspended for a time.
On heavy wings, ringed pheasants rose
At our approach.
The fields were yellow with mustard,
Parrots wheeled in the sunshine, dipped
    and disappeared
Into the morning mist on the foothills.
We found a pool, fed by a freshet
Of cold spring water. 'One day when we are men,'
He said, 'We'll meet here at the pool again.
Promise?' 'Promise,' I said. And we took a pledge,
In blood, nicking our fingers on a penknife
And pressing them to each other's lips. Sweet,
    salty kiss.
Late evening, past cowdust time, we trudged home:
He to his mother, I to my dinner.

One wining-dancing night I thought I'd stay
    out too.
We went to the pictures—*Gone with the Wind*—
A crashing bore for boys, and it finished late.
So I had dinner with them, and his mother said:
'It's past ten. You'd better stay the night.
But will they miss you?'

I did not answer but climbed into my friend's
    bed—
I'd never slept with anyone before, except
    my father—
And when it grew cold, after midnight,
He put his arms around me and looped a leg
Over mine and it was nice that way
But I stayed awake with the niceness of it
My sleep stolen by his own deep slumber...
What dreams were lost, I'll never know!
But next morning, just as we'd started breakfast,
A car drew up, and my parents, outraged,
Chastized me for staying out and hustled me home.
Breakfast unfinished. My friend unhappy. My
    pride wounded.
We met sometimes, but a constraint had grown
    upon us,
And the following month I heard he'd gone
To an orphanage in Kalimpong.

4

I remember you well, old banyan tree,
As you stood there spreading quietly
Over the broken wall.
While adults slept, I crept away
Down the broad veranda steps, around
The outhouse and the melon-ground...
In that winter of long ago, I roamed
The faded garden of my mother's home.

I must have known that giants have few friends
(The great lurk shyly in their private dens),
And found you hidden by a thick green wall
Of aerial roots.
Intruder in your pillared den, I stood
And shyly touched your old and wizened wood,
And as my heart explored you, giant tree,
I heard you singing!

The spirit of the tree became my friend,
Took me to his silent throbbing heart
And taught me the value of stillness!
My first tutor; friend of the lonely.

And the second was the tonga-man
Whose pony-cart came rattling along the road
Under the furthest arch of the banyan tree.
Looking up, he waved his whip at me

And laughing, called, 'Who lives up there?'
'I do,' I said.
And the next time he came along, he stopped
    the tonga
And asked me if I felt lonely in the tree.
'Only sometimes,' I said. 'When the tree
    is thinking.'
'I never think,' he said. 'You won't feel lonely
    with me.'
And with a flick of the reins he rattled away,
With a promise he'd give me a ride someday.
And from him I learnt the value of promises kept.

5

From the tree to the tonga was an easy drop.
I fell into life. Bansi, tonga-driver,
Wore a yellow waistcoat and spat red
Betel-juice the entire width of the road.
'I can spit further than any man,' he claimed.
It is natural for a man to strive to excel
At something; he spat with authority.

When he took me for rides, he lost a fare.
That was his way. He once said, 'If a girl
Wants five rupees for a fix, bargain like hell
And then give six.'
It was the secret of his failure, he claimed,
To give away more than he owned.

And to prove it, he borrowed my pocket money
In order to buy a present for his mistress.

A man who fails well is better than one who
    succeeds badly.

The rattletrap tonga and the winding road
Through the valley, to the riverbed,
With the wind in my hair and the dust
Rising, and the dogs running and barking

And Bansi singing and shouting in my ear,
And the pony farting as it cantered along,
Wheels creaking, seat shifting,
Hood slipping off, the entire contraption
Always about to disintegrate, collapse,
But never quite doing so—like the man himself…
All this was music,
And the ragtime-raga lingers in my mind.

Nostalgia comes swiftly when one is forty,
Looking back at boyhood years.
Even unhappiness acquires a certain glow.

It was shady in the cemetery, and the mango trees
Did well there, nourished by the bones
Of long-dead Colonels, Collectors, Magistrates
    and Memsahibs.

For here, in dusty splendour, lay the graves
Of those who'd brought their English dust
To lie with Ganges soil: some tombs were temples,
Some were cenotaphs; and one, a tiny Taj.
Here lay sundry relatives, including Uncle Henry,
Who'd been for many years a missionary.
'Sacred to the Memory
Of Henry C. Wagstaff',
Who translated the Gospels into Pashtu,
And was murdered by his own chowkidar.

'Well done, thou good and faithful servant'—
So ran his epitaph.

The gardener, who looked after the trees,
Also dug graves. One day
I found him working at the bottom of a
    new cavity,
They never let me know in time,' he grumbled.
'Last week I dug two graves, and now,
    without warning,
Here's another. It isn't even the season for dying.
There's enough work all summer, when
    cholera's about—
Why can't they keep alive through the winter?'
Near the railway lines, watching the trains
(There were six every day, coming or going),

And across the line, the leper colony…
I did not know they were lepers till later
But I knew they were different: some
Were without fingers or toes
And one had no nose
And a few had holes in their faces
And yet some were beautiful.
They had their children with them
And the children were no different
From other children.
I made friends with some
And won most of their marbles
And carried them home in my pockets.

One day my parents found me
Playing near the leper colony.
There was a big scene.
My mother shouted at the lepers
And they hung their heads as though it was all
    their fault,
And the children had nothing to say.
I was taken home in disgrace
And told all about leprosy and given a bath.
My clothes were thrown away
And the servants wouldn't touch me for days.
So I took the marbles I'd won
And put them in my stepfather's cupboard,
Hoping he'd catch leprosy from them.

6

A slim dark youth with quiet
Eyes and a gentle quizzical smile,
Manohar. Fifteen, working in a small hotel.
He'd come from the hills and wanted to return.
I forget how we met
But I remember walking the dusty roads
With this gentle boy, who held my hand
And told me about his home, his mother,
His village, and the little river
At the bottom of the hill where the water
Ran blue and white and wonderful,
'When I go home, I'll take you with me.'
But we hadn't enough money.
So I sold my bicycle for thirty rupees
And left a note in the dining room:
'Going away. Don't worry—(hoping they would)—
I'll come home
When I've grown up.'

We crossed the rushing waters of the Ganga
Where they issued from the doors of Vishnu,
Then took the pilgrim road, in those days
Just a stony footpath into the mountains:
Not all who ventured forth returned;
Some came to die, of course,
Near the sacred waters or at their source.
We took this route and spent a night

At a wayside inn, wrapped tight
In the single blanket I'd brought along;
Even then we were cold
It was not the season for pilgrims
And the inn was empty, except for the locals
Drinking a local brew.

We drank a little and listened
To an old soldier from the hills
Talking of the women he'd known
In the first Great War, when stationed in Rome;
His memories were good for many drinks
In many inns; his face pickled in the suns
Of many mountain summers.
The mule-drivers slept in one room
And talked all night over hookahs.
Manohar slept bravely, but I lay watching
A bright star through the tiny window
And wished upon it, already knowing that wishes
Had no power, but wishing all the same…
And next morning we set off again
Leaving the pilgrim route to march
Down a valley, above a smaller river,
Walking until I felt
We'd walk and walk for ever.
Late at night, on a cold mountain,
Two lonely figures, we saw the lights
Of scattered houses and knew we had arrived.

7

'Not death, but a summing-up of life,'
Said the village patriarch, as we watched him
Treasure a patch of winter sunshine
On his string cot in the courtyard.
I remember his wisdom.
And I remember faces.
For it's faces I remember best.
The people were poor, and the patriarch said:
'I have heard it told that the sun
Sets in splendour in Himalaya—
But who can eat sunsets?'

Perhaps, if I'd stayed longer,
I would have yearned for creature comforts.
We were hungry sometimes, eating wild berries
Or slyly milking another's goat,
Or catching small fish in the river…
But I did not long for home.
Could I have grown up a village boy,
Grazing sheep and cattle, while the Collected Works
Of W. Shakespeare lay gathering dust
In Dehra? Who knows? But it was nice
Of my stepfather to send his office manager
Into the mountains to bring me home!

Manohar.
He called goodbye and waved
As I looked back from the bend in the road.
Bright boy on the mountainside,
Waving to me, calling, and I've loved you
All these years and looked for you everywhere,
In the mountains, in crowds at distant places,
In cities and villages, beside the sea.
And the trains roll on, every day
Hundreds of people coming or going or
    running away—
Goodbye, goodbye!
Into the forest's silence,
Outside the dark tunnel,
Out of the tunnel, out of the dark…

Written at Maplewood, 1970.

Going Home

On the road to the Delhi, five hours
    of listening
To the taxi-driver proclaiming
The virtues of his loud new horn,
Kept me from dwelling too long on
    the approaching
Face of my lost mother, her dying
Remembering eyes, or the reproach
Of her last dark glance when I turned and left
    the house
Oh, many years ago; the final wrench,
That last acknowledgement from her.

I Was the Wind Last Night

(For my adopted grandson, Rakesh, when he was very small and was taken to his village by his parents)

> I was the wind last night.
> I vaulted the river and swam seven mountains.
> And turned aside the tall trees guarding the valley.
> I caught glimpses of you through the window as I
>   wandered around the little house.
> They would not let me in; too cold a wind!
> I hung around listlessly, afraid to call too loud.
> Then like a weary man limped homewards over
>   the sleeping mountains.
> When will I learn the value of stillness?

Lullaby

(For Rakesh when he was very small)

> Little one, don't be afraid of this big river.
> Be safe in these warm arms for ever.
> Grow tall, my son, be wise and strong,
> But do not take from any man his song.
> Little one, don't be afraid of this dark night.
> Walk boldly as you see the truth and light.
> Love well, my son, laugh all day long,
> But do not take from any man his song.

Summer Fruit

Summer is here, and mangoes too
And fruit of every taste and hue;
And given a choice of juice or berry,
I'll settle for the humble cherry.
I know your favourite on this planet
Is the red and rosy pomegranate;
But that's a winter fruit, my child,
So wait until the weather's mild.
But if you like a simple khana,
There's nothing like a good banana.
No? Something more exotic?
Maybe some lichis in your pockets.
Or would you like a large tarbuj—
It's sweeter than a good kharbuj—
Tarbuj, kharbuj—oh, what's the difference?
Tell me, children, and your preference.

Granny's Tree-climbing

My grandmother was a genius. You'd like to
    know why?
Because she could climb trees. Spreading or high,
She'd be up their branches in a trice. And
    mind you,
When last she climbed a tree, she was sixty-two.
Ever since childhood, she'd had this gift
For being happier in a tree than in a lift;
And though, as years went by, she would be told
That climbing trees should stop when one
    grew old—
And that growing old should be gone
    about gracefully—
She'd laugh and say, 'Well, I'll grow
    old disgracefully.
I can do it better.' And we had to agree;
For in all the garden there wasn't a tree
She hadn't been up, at one time or another
(Having learned to climb from a loving brother
When she was six)—but it was feared by all
That one day she'd have a terrible fall.
The outcome was different—while we were in town

She climbed a tree and couldn't come down.
After the rescue,
The doctor took Granny's temperature and said,
'I strongly recommend a quiet week in bed.'
We sighed with relief and tucked her up well.
Poor Granny! For her, it was like a brief season in hell,
Confined to her bedroom, while every breeze
Whispered of summer and dancing leaves.
But she held her peace till she felt stronger,
Then sat up and said, 'I'll lie here no longer!'
And she called for my father and told him undaunted
That a house in a tree-top was what she now wanted.
My Dad knew his duties. He said, 'That's all right—
You'll have what you want, dear. I'll start work tonight.'
With my expert assistance, he soon finished the chore:
Made her a tree-house with windows and a door.
So Granny moved up, and now every day
I climb to her room with glasses and a tray.
She sits there in state and drinks sherry with me,
Upholding her right to reside in a tree.

What Can We Give Our Children?

What can we give our children?
Knowledge, yes, and honour too,
And strength of character
And the gift of laughter.
What gold do we give our children?
The gold of a sunny childhood,
Open spaces, a home that binds
Us to the common good…
These simple things
Are greater than the gold of kings.

Don't Be Afraid of the Dark

Don't be afraid of the dark, little one,
The earth must rest when the day is done.
The sun may be harsh, but moonlight—never!
And those stars will be shining forever and ever,
Be friends with the Night, there is nothing to fear,
Just let your thoughts travel to friends far and near.
By day, it does seem that our troubles won't cease,
But at night, late at night, the world is at peace.

View from the Window

I'm in bed with fever
But the fever's not high.
Beside my bed is a window
And I like looking out at all
That's happening around me.
The cherry leaves are turning a dark green.
On the maple tree, winged seeds spin round
    and round.
There is fruit on the wild blackberry bushes.
Two mynah birds are building a nest in a hole—
They are very noisy about it.
Bits of grass keep falling on the window sill.
High up in the spruce tree, a hawk-cuckoo calls:
'I slept so well, I slept so well!'
When the hawk-cuckoo is awake, no one
    else sleeps,
That's why it's also known as the fever bird.
A small squirrel climbs on the window sill.
He's been coming every day since I've been ill,
and I give him crumbs from my tray.
A boy on a mule passes by on the rough
    mountain track.
He sees my face at the window and waves to me.
I wave back to him.
When I'm better I'll ask him to let me ride
    his mule.

Boy in a Blue Pullover

Boy in a faded blue pullover,
Poor boy, thin, smiling boy,
Ran down the road shouting,
Singing, flinging his arms wide.
I stood in the way and stopped him.
'What's up?' I said. 'Why are you happy?'
He showed me the nickel rupee-coin.
'I found it on the road,' he said.
And he held it to the light
That he might see it shining bright.
'And how will you spend it,
Small boy in blue pullover?'
'I'll buy—
I'll buy a buckle for my belt!'
Slim boy, smart boy,
Would buy a buckle for his belt
Coin clutched in his hot hand,
He ran off laughing, bright.
The coin I'd lost an hour ago;
But better his that night.

To Live in Magic

What more perfect friend
    than the friend you have given me, Lord;
What more perfect song than the
    whistling-thrush at dawn's first light;
What lovelier thing than the ladybird
    opening its wings on the rose-petal;
What greater gift than this moment in time,
    this heart-beat in the night?

October

October comes…
The mountains resonate
To festive drums.
At sunset time
The western sky
Is drenched
A crimson winterline.
October's here.
The pilgrims come
Steep hills to climb,
For now
It's Durga-puja time.

At Ganga's mouth
The icy waters
Issue forth.
The hills resound
As waters from the north
Sweep down…
The mighty river
Makes its way
And winds along

To Bangla's Bay.

The days speed by,
Diwali lamps
Are shining forth
From East and West
And South and North.
The goddess smiles,
Our heads bow down,
We pray
For better things to come.

October's gone!
The nights grow long,
We sing a softer
Sadder song,
Recalling hopes of yesterday,
Lost loves, lost dreams…
But still we pray
For better times to come our way.

Granny's Proverbs

A hungry man is an angry man,
Said dear old Gran
As she prepared an Irish stew
For the chosen few
(Gran'dad, my cousins and me).
But then she'd turn to me and emote—
'Don't be greedy, or your tongue will cut your
 throat!'
And if I asked for more of my favourite fish,
'That small fish,' she'd say, 'is better than an
 empty dish!'
Like Manu, she taught us to honour our food,
She was the law-giver, seeking all good.
Gran'dad and I, we'd eat what we were given
(Irish stew and a tart)
But sometimes we'd sneak away to the bazaar
To feast on tikkees and chaat
—And that was heaven!

We Rode All the Way to Delhi

In the Bicycle Age
When I was a kid
We rode all the way to Delhi,
Yes we did!
Somi and Ranji and I…
It took us three days
As we pressed on our pedals,
All two hundred miles
From Dehra to Delhi,
And they gave us no medals!
We sheltered in dhabas
And ate what they gave us,
But no welcoming crowd
In Delhi received us
As dusty, dishevelled
We crossed the old bridge
And rode round the city
And camped on the Ridge.

Next day we rose late—
Our bodies they ached—
So instead of cycling

All the way back again
We put our bikes on the train
And went home in style
To Dehra from Delhi,
Somi and Ranji and I…

My Best Friend

My best Friend
Is the baker's son,
I gave him a book
And he gave me a bun!

I told him a tale
Of a magical lake,
And he liked it so much
That he baked me a cake.

Yes, he's my best friend—
We go cycling together,
On bright sunny days,
Or in rain and bad weather.

And if we feel hungry
There's always a pie
Or a pastry to feast on,
As we go riding by!

This commemorates a small bakery in the old Dilaram Bazaar area during my boyhood in Dehra.

It Isn't Time That's Passing

Remember the long ago when we lay together
In a pain of tenderness and counted
Our dreams: long summer afternoons
When the whistling-thrush released
A deep sweet secret on the trembling air;
Blackbird on the wing, bird of the forest shadows,
Black rose in the long ago summer,
This was your song:
It isn't time that's passing by,
It is you and I.

Love Lyrics for Binya Devi

1

Your face streamed April rain,
As you climbed the steep hill,
Calling the white cow home.
You seemed very tiny
On the windswept mountainside;
A twist of hair lay
Strung across your forehead
And your torn blue skirt
Clung to your tender thighs.
You smiled through the blind white rain
And gave me the salt kiss of your lips,
Salt mingled with raindrop and mint,
And left me there, where I had come to
    fetch you—
So gallant in the blistering rain!
And you ran home laughing;
But it was worth the drenching.

2

Your feet, laved with dew,
Stood firm on the quickening grass.

There was a butterfly between us:
Red and gold its wings
And heavy with dew.
It could not move because of the weight
    of moisture.
And as your foot came nearer
And I saw that you would crush it,
I said: 'Stay. It has only a few days
In the sun, and we have many.'
'And if I spare it,' you said, laughing.
'What will you do for me, what will you pay?'
'Why, anything you say.'
'And will you kiss my foot?'
'Both feet,' I said; and did so happily.
For they were no less than the wings of butterflies.

3

All night our love
Stole sleep from dusty eyes.
What dreams were lost, I'll never know.
It seemed the world's last night had come
And there would never be a dawn.

Your touch soon swept the panting dark away—
Some suns are brighter by night than day!

4

Your eyes, glad and wondering,
Dwelt in mine,

And all that stood between us
Was a blade of grass
Shivering slightly
In the breath from our lips.
But grass will bend.
We turn and kiss,
And the world swings round,
The sky spins, the trees go hush
Hush, the mountain sings—
Though we must leave this place,
We've trapped forever
In the trembling air
The last sweet phantom kiss.

5

I know you'll come when the cherries
Are ripe;
But it is still November
And I must wait
For the green fruit to blush
At your approach.
And meanwhile the tree is visited
By robber bands, masked mynas
And yellow birds with beaks like daggers,
Determined not to leave one cherry
Whole for lovers.
But still I wait, hoping one day
You'll come to stain your lips

With cherry-juice, and climb my tree;
Bright goddess in your dark green temple,
Thrusting your tongue at me.

6

Slender waisted, bright as a song,
Dark as the whistling-thrush at dawn,
Swift as the running days of November,
Lost like a dream too sweet to remember.

The Love of Two Stars

Two stars fell in love. Between them came sky
And ten moons and two suns riding high,
Before them the nebulous star-crusted Way,
The silence of Night, the silver of Day.
A million years passed, the lovers still glowed
With the brilliance and fire and passion of old;
But one star grew restless and set off at night
With a wonderful shower of hot white light.
He sped to his love, with his hopes and his fears,
But missed her, alas, by a thousand light-years.

Lovers Observed

Lovers lie drowsy in the grass,
Sunk in bracken, swimming in pools
Of late afternoon sunshine;
All agitation past, they stay totally
Absorbed in grass.

Green grass, and growing from that place
A sweep of languid arm still bare
But for a lost ladybird.
Anonymous lover brushes a dragon
Fly from his face.

Brief thunder blossoms in the air,
A leaf between the thighs is caught
And crushed. Love comes like a thief,
Crouching among the bruised and broken clover.
All flesh in grass.

Phantom Lover

Night unto night
When the world's asleep,
You come to me,
Our tryst to keep.
Held captive, in thrall,
As the stars look down,
Body and soul
From night unto dawn.
Silent you come
And softly you go,
Ours is a love
That none must know.

We Must Keep Loving, All Our Days

We must love someone.
We must keep loving, all our days,
Someone, anyone, anywhere
Outside our selves;
For even the sarus crane
Will grieve over its lost companion,
And the seal its mate.
Somewhere in life
There must be someone
To take your hand
And share the torrid day.
Without the touch of love
There is no life, and we must fade away.

Primrose Hill

She held my hand on Primrose Hill,
I loved her then and love her still.
Although she had sworn we never would part
She went away with the shreds of my heart.
But I loved her then and love her still,
And I see her still climbing up Primrose Hill.

Passing By

Enough for me that you are beautiful:
Beauty possessed diminishes.
Better a dream of love
Than love's dream broken;
Better a look exchanged
Than love's word spoken.
Enough for me that you walk past,
A firefly flashing in the dark.

Love's Sad Song

There's a sweet little girl lives down the lane,
And she's so pretty and I'm so plain,
She's clever and smart and all things good,
And I'm the bad boy of the neighbourhood.
But I'd be her best friend forever and a day
If only she'd smile and look my way.

Love Is a Law

Who shall set a law to lovers?
Love is a law unto itself

Love gained is often lost
And love that's lost is found again

It's love that makes the world go round
Love that keeps us closely bound

Take this power to love away
We would be just beasts of prey

If Love should lose its hold on us
Discord would rule the Universe.

One Flower

It has bloomed again,
This flower that I thought dead.
In one moment of despair
And pain,
I'd trampled it in the ground
Upon this barren plain.
Little did I know
That it would rise again,
This flower that I thought dead.
My soul would need
A surer weapon than despair
To crush a thing so bright, so fair.

Listen!

Listen to the night wind in the trees,
Listen to the summer grass singing;
Listen to the time that's tripping by,
And the dawn dew falling.
Listen to the moon as it climbs the sky,
Listen to the pebbles humming;
Listen to the mist in the trembling leaves,
And the silence calling.

Rain in the Hills

In the hushed silence of the house
when I am quite alone, and my friend, who
    was here,
has gone, it is very lonely, very quiet,
as I sit in a liquid silence, a silence within,
surrounded by the rhythm of rain
the steady drift
of water on leaves, on lemons, on roof,
drumming on drenched dahlias and window panes,
while the mist holds the house in a dark caress.

As I pause near a window, the rain stops.
And starts again.
And the trees, no longer green but grey,
menace me with their loneliness.

This was the first poem I wrote when I came to live in the hills, 1963.

Night Thoughts

This mountain is my mother,
My father is the sea,
This river is the fountain
Of all that life may be…
Swift river from the mountain,
Deep river to the sea,
Take all my words and leave them
Where the west wind sets them free.
So, piper on the lonely hill,
Play no sad songs for me;
The day has gone, sweet night comes on,
Its darkness helps me see.

Out of the Darkness

Out of darkness we came, into darkness we go,
Out of the sea to the land we know,
Out of the trembling hills and its streams,
From night unto day we come with our dreams.

The wind and the water gave form to our lives;
After thousands of aeons mankind still survives,
And beyond those great spaces, those planets
 and stars,
Who knows, there are heart-beats and children
 like ours.

Wild Is the Wind

Wild is the wind tonight,
Deep is the thunder,
Lightning across the sky
Splits it asunder.
Witches will ride tonight,
Ranging the sky,
Wizards will cast their spells—
Great men will die.
Who'll be my guide tonight,
Starless the sky;
Who'll brave the demons
Now riding so high.
I'll take the road alone,
I'll reach my goal;
Witches and wizards
Must yield to man's soul.

A Quiet Mind

Lord, give me a quiet mind,
That I might listen;
A gentle tone of voice,
That I might comfort others;
A sound and healthy body,
That I might share
In the joy of walking
And leaping and running;
And a good sense of direction
So I might know just where I'm going!

Lone Fox Dancing

As I walked home last night
I saw a lone fox dancing
In the cold moonlight.

I stood and watched. Then
Took the low road, knowing
The night was his by right.

Sometimes, when words ring true,
I'm like a lone fox dancing
In the morning dew.

The Bat

Most bats fly high,
Swooping only
To take some insect on the wing;
But there's a bat I know
Who flies so low
He skims the floor;
He does not enter at the window
But flies in at the door,
Does stunts beneath the furniture…
Is his radar wrong,
Or does he just prefer
Being different from other bats?
And when sometimes
He settles upside down
At the foot of my bed,
I let him be.
On lonely nights, even a crazy bat
Is company.

This commemorates the Jhanpani bat who used to visit me at Maplewood, Mussoorie.

Firefly in My Room

Last night, as I lay sleepless
In the summer dark
With window open to invite a breeze,
Softly a firefly flew in
And circled round the room
Twinkling at me from floor or wall
Or ceiling, never long in one place
But lighting up little spaces…
A friendly presence, dispelling
The settled gloom of an unhappy day.

And after it had gone, I left
The window open, just in case
It should return.

For Silence

Thank you, Lord, for silence;
The silence of great mountains
and deserts and forests.
For the silence of the street
late at night
when the last travellers
are safely home
and the traffic is still.
For the silence in my room
in which I can hear small sounds outside:
a moth fluttering against the window pane,
the drip of the dew running off the roof,
and a field mouse rustling through dry leaves.

In This Workaday World

It's a busy world, I know,
And we must hurry here and there
And not ask who or why or where,
For fear our credits fall too low.
But here upon this hilly crest
There's some respite; and when
The fretting day is done,
Beneath the cherry tree there's rest.

Evening by the Fireside

Boy by the fire dreaming
Baby sleeping
Mother nodding, knitting
Father reading
Wood crackling, spitting
Wind in the chimney humming
Old house creaking
Small mouse squeaking
No one speaking…

Baby waking!
Boy hungry
Mother grumbly
Father rumbly-bumbly
Baby shrieking!
Old house shaking
Small mouse squeaking
Wind in chimney howling
Everyone shouting, scowling
Baby *yowling*!

Written during a wintry evening with the family in Landour.

Cricket-Field Placings

Long leg has a cramp in one leg,
Short leg has a cramp in two;
Twelfth man is fielding at mid-off,
Because mid-on's gone off to the loo.
As short square leg has a long leg,
Long-off has been moved further off;
Silly-point goes back to gully
Cover-point backs off a pace or two.
Everyone is thinking of the drinks' trolley
When first slip lets a catch through his fingers,
Forgetting the old ball is now new.

A Plea for Bowlers

Cricket never will be fair
Till bowlers get their rightful share
For toiling in the midday sun.
What should be done?
It's simple—
Make those wickets broader, taller!
That should make it much more fun
For the poor perspiring bowler.

P.S. And in the interests of the game
The size of the bat remains the same.

Foot Soldiers

'Where's Solan?' the private was asking.
'Somewhere in Tibet, I should think.'
'There's a brewery there.
And it's brimming with beer,
But we can't get a mouthful to drink!'

So we route-march from Delhi to Solan
In the dust and the devilish sun,
And we're cursing away like Hades,
'Cause there ain't any ladies
To hear every son-of-a-gun!

And when we have climbed up to Solan
Our language continues profane,
For right well we know
We shall soon have to go.
Down from Solan to Delhi again.

Written as a tribute to my soldier grandfather.

Song for a Beetle

A beetle fell into the goldfish bowl,
Hey-ho!
The beetle began to struggle and roll,
Ho-hum!
The window was open, the moon shone bright,
The crickets were singing with all their might,
But a blundering beetle had muddled his flight
And here he was now, in a watery plight,
Having given the goldfish a terrible fright,
Ho-hum, hey-ho!

The beetle swam left, the beetle swam right,
Hum-ho!
Along came myself—I said, 'Lord, what a sight!
That poor old beetle will drown tonight.'
Ho-hum.
A beetle is just an insect, I hear,
But what if I fell in a vat full of beer?
I'd be brewed to light lager if no one came near—
(It happened, I'm told, to a man in Ajmer)—
Ho-hum, ho-hum.

With my fingers and thumb
The beetle I seized;
The goldfish were pleased!
The window was open, the moon shone bright,
I flung that beetle far out in the night,
And he bumbled away in a staggering flight,
Ho-hum, hey-ho,
Good night!

I think I'd enjoyed a couple of rums before I wrote this one!

The Cat Has Something to Say

Sir, you're a human and I'm a cat,
And I'm really quite happy to leave it at that.
It doesn't concern me if you like a dish
Of chicken masala or lobster and fish.
So why all these protests around the house
If for dinner I fancy
A succulent mouse?
Or a careless young sparrow who came my way?
Our natures, dear sir, are really the same:
Flesh, fish or fowl, we both like our game.
Only you take yours curried,
And I take mine plain.

Written for Suzi, or Souza, my Siamese cat.

A Nightmare

Cupid, with his famous dart,
Struck me just above the heart—
'Life' he said, 'is just a gamble,
You'll take to her without preamble.
And so there came, all bent and grey,
This withered crone, and she did sway
Backwards and forwards, as though she'd seen
The phantom lover of a dream.
She hypnotised me with one glance
And there and then began to dance,
Then tossed me in her waiting carriage
And promised me her hand in marriage.
She took me to her home in state,
And chortling, said, 'There's no escape,
I'll keep you in my empty cupboard;
You know my name—it's Mother Hubbard!
I'll feed you frogs and make you fat—
A kofta for my favourite cat.'
Her cat? The thing she called her darling
Was a monstrous tiger, fiercely snarling,
Its eyes were burning bright and red.
It pounced! I woke up in my bed.
No tiger lady in my cupboard…
But when I opened my front door
I found the brass plate bore
My name: Mr Hubbard.

Hip-Hop Nature Boy

When I was seven,
And climbing trees,
I stepped into a hive of bees.
Badly stung and mad with pain,
I danced the hip-hop in the rain.
Hip-hop, I'm a nature boy,
Mother Nature's pride and joy!

When I was twelve,
Still climbing trees,
I fell instead—
And landed on my head.
Feeling lighter,
I thought I might become a writer.
Hip-hop, dancing in the rain,
A nature-writer I became!

With Nature being my natural bent,
At twenty I took out my tent,
And spent the night beside a Nadi,
Wearing only vest and chuddee.
At crack of drawn I woke to find

A crocodile was close behind,
And smiling broadly!

In times of crises at my best,
I did not trouble to get dressed,
But fled towards the Gulf of Kutch,
With fond salaams to muggermuch!
Mother Nature once again
Found me dancing on the plain,
Nanga-panga in the rain!

Growing older, even bolder,
Took a winding mountain trail,
Up a hill and down a dale,
All to see a mountain-quail.

The quail was extinct, long expired,
I was limping, very tired,
Thought I saw a comfy cot
In the corner of a hut.
Feeling grateful, I sank down
Upon a blanket soft as down.
Blanket rose up all at once,
Gave a shudder, then a pounce.
Stumbling in the darkness there,
I'd disturbed a big brown bear!

I did not stop to say goodnight,

But fled into the open night.
Hip-hop in the rain,
Dancing to that old refrain.

Growing old, I thought it safer
In my tryst with Mother Nature,
To grow flowers—
Roses, dahlias,
Poppies, sweet peas, rare azaleas,
Candy tuft and tiny tansies,
Violets sweet and naughty pansies…
A lovely garden I'd constructed,
Birds and bees were soon inducted.

Bees! Did I say bees?
They were buzzing all around me—
Angry, diving down upon me,
For where their hive had been suspended,
By accident it lay upended!

Dear Reader, if you must
In Nature put your trust,
Stay away from swarms of bees
And strange crocs lurking under trees,
Or else, like me, you'll dance with pain
While doing the hip-hop in the rain.

In Praise of the Sausage

I like a good sausage, I do;
It's a dish for the chosen and few.
Oh, for sausage and mash,
And of mustard a dash,
And an egg nicely fried—maybe two?
At breakfast or lunch, or at dinner,
The sausage is always a winner;
If you want a good spread
Go for sausage on bread,
And forget all your vows to be slimmer.

If Mice Could Roar

If mice could roar
And elephants soar
And trees grow up in the sky,
If tigers could dine
On biscuits and wine,
And the fattest of men could fly!
If pebbles could sing
And bells never ring
And teachers get lost in the post:
If a tortoise could run
And losses be won,
And bullies be buttered on toast;
If a song brought a shower,
And a gun grew a flower,
This world would be nicer than most!

Night Rhyme

Gobble-gobble said the turkey,
Honk-honk said the goose.
Cluck-cluck said the little hen,
Squeak-squeak said the mouse.
Clang-clang went our motor-car;
Bang-bang went the wedding band.
Katar-katar went the porcupine,
Tootle-tootle went the train.
Nothing-nothing said the goldfish,
And the earthworm said the same.
Sleep tight, says Ayah-papaya,
And God protect my little baba.

This is the first poem I ever wrote.

The Demon Driver

At driving a car I've never been good—
I batter the bumper and damage the hood—
'Get off the road!' the traffic cops shout,
'You're supposed to go *round* that roundabout!'
'I thought it was quicker to drive straight through.'
'Give us your license—it's time to renew.'
I took their advice and handed a fee
To a Babu who looked on this windfall with glee.
'No problem,' he said, 'Your license now pukka,
You may drive all the way from here to Kolkata.'

So away I drove, at a feverish pitch,
Advancing some way down an unseen ditch.
Once back on the highway, I soon joined the fray
Of hundreds of drivers who wouldn't give way:
I skimmed past a truck and revolved round a van
(Good drivers can do anything that they can)
Then offered a lift to a man with a load—
'Just a little way down to the end of this road.'
As I pressed on the pedal, the car gave a shudder:
He'd got in at one door, got out at the other.
'God help you!' he said, as he hurried away,

'I'll come for a drive another fine day!'
I came to that roundabout, round it I sped
Eager to get to my dinner and bed.
Round it I went, and round it once more
'Get off the road!' That cop was a bore.
I swung to the left and went clean through a wall,
My neighbour stood there—he looked
    menacing, tall—
'This will cost you three thousand,' he quietly said,
'And send me your cheque before you're in bed!'
Alas! my new car was sent for repair,
But my friends gathered round and said, never
    despair!
'We are all going to help you to make a fresh start.'
And next day they gave me a nice bullock-cart.

This commemorates my struggle to drive a Land Rover in New Delhi, many years ago.

Do You Believe in Ghosts?

'Do you believe in ghosts?'
Asked the passenger
On platform number three.
'I'm a rational man,' said I,
'I believe in what I can see—
Your hands, your feet, your beard!'
Then look again,' said he,
And promptly disappeared!

In a Strange Cafe

Waiter, where's my soup?
On its way, sir, loop the loop!
Straight from our famous cooking pot,
Here it comes, sir, piping hot!

But waiter, there's a fly in my soup.
That's no fly, sir,
That's your chicken.
The smaller the chicken, the better the soup!

Please take it away.
I'll just have the curry and a plate of rice…
The curry's very good, sir, full of spice!
Waiter, what's this object that's floating around?
Just a small beetle, sir,
Homeward bound!

Never mind the curry, just bring me some bread,
I have to eat something before I'm in bed.
What's on the menu? Hungarian Goulash?
I suppose it's served up with beetles and mash.
Isn't there anything else I can eat?

Yes sir, you could try the crow's feet.
Highly recommended and good for the teeth.

All our best guests
Are most happily fed here.
And where are they now?
All happily dead, sir.

And So To Bed

In bed we lie, in bed we sleep,
In bed we laugh, in bed we weep;
In bed we groan when racked with pain,
And when we're well we smile again.
In bed we toss, in bed we snore,
We wake up late, then sleep some more.
In bed we scratch, in bed we curse
If bugs abound, or something worse!
In bed we dream, in bed we mope,
 We sigh but never give up hope.
In bed we're born, in bed we die,
Unless, of course, we climb a peak
And from it fall a thousand feet!
Most of your life is spent in bed—
A horizontal man, much better than
One standing stiff with unsupported head.
Respect your bed, my friend,
It's there beside you till the end.
So keep it soft, and keep it neat,
And may God bless your tired feet.

The Good for Nothing

You may rush for your bus, but I—
I still linger with my dreams,
And watch the sunlight stalk the shadows on
    the wall

You may pound your machines,
But I am more concerned about the leaves
    that fall

Restlessly, rustling down the garden path.
And the dew-drops caught in a spider's web
Are more precious to me
Than pearls clustering a silken throat.
I fish without bait:
I do not get anything on my line;
But it is a good reason for doing nothing for a
    long time.

September Morn

September morn, and autumn's here again,
Soft sunshine celebrates departing rain.
Wild flowers now make their gentle
    presence known,
Small children pluck them as they wander home.
The grass smells sweet, the birds interrogate
Each other in the trees. And I'm late
And miss my business date in town,
No matter. I'll take that loan another day.
I'll climb the hill today!
This golden morn is interest-free,
And there is none to punish me.

Who'll Buy My Poems?

Who'll buy my poems?
I sang out to the silent stones.
And came the dread reply
In deep sepulchral tones:
We'll buy your eyes
We'll buy your heart and bones
We'll buy your rags
And settle all your loans
But please don't send us any poems,
We will not buy your rotten poems!

Secondhand Shop in Hill Station

The smell of secondhand goods
Is everywhere. Lost causes,
Lonely lives, and deaths in small cottages
Among the pines, meet here in the
    mildewed dark
Of his shop—Abdul Salaam, Proprietor.
Tales of a hundred failures
And ten hundred broken dreams.

A hat-pin and an Iron Cross
Lie down with a blackened pistol,
While a bronze Buddha smiles across
At a plastic doll from Bristol.

Old clothes, old books (perhaps a first edition?),
A dressing-gown, a dagger marked with rust.
A card for some lost Christmas,
And inside, a letter:
'Dear Jane, I am getting better.'
A Chinese vase and a china-dog.

The shop is cold and thick with dust,
The Mall is far from grand;
But Abdul Salaam grows prosperous,
In a suit that's secondhand.

Lost All My Money

I've lost all my money,
And I'm on my way home;
Home to the hills and a field full of rocks.
Nothing in the city but a sickness of the soul,
Nothing to earn but sorrow…
I've lost all my money
And I'm on my way home,
With nothing to buy my way home…
I've lost all my money
And I can't bribe the guard,
So help me, O Lord,
On my way home…

We Are the Babus

Soak the rich and harry the poor,
That's our motto and our law;
We are the rulers of this land,
We are the babus, a merry band,
Under the table, or through the back door,
We'll empty your pockets and ask for more!
We are the babus, this is our law—
Soak the rich and harry the poor!

Slum Children at Play

Imps of mischief,
Barefoot in the dust,
Grinning, mocking, even as
They beg you for a crust.
No angels these,
Just hungry eyes
And eager hands
To help you sympathize…
They don't want love,
They don't seek pity,
They know there's nothing
In this heartless city
But a kindred need
In those who strive
For power and pelf
Though only just alive!
They know your guilt,
They'll take your money,
And if you give too much
They'll find you funny.
Because that's what you are—
You're just a joke—

Your life is soft
And theirs all grime and smoke
And yet they shout and sing
And do not thank your giving,
You'll fuss and fret through life
While they do all the living.

Home from the Burning-Ghat

All the way home from the burning-ghat
I saw dead men in the streets their skulls
Bleached white their smiles already ashes,
I saw worms in the eyes of children
And green fungi growing from the feet
Of old men.   A clear September day.

The windows were open. Garlands of
Marigolds blazed outside and a voice
Remote on the ether said, 'Racing.
The horse Nijinsky has recovered
From an attack of American
Ringworm, and will be running today.'

Dragonflies

These are the painted people,
Living in mean streets
Behind the shadowed walls
Of the old city—
The young-old hermaphrodites—
Their lives transparent
As the green-gold wings
Of summer dragonflies.
These are the laughing people,
Whose shattered lusts
Each day grow more omnivorous.

Midwinter, Deserted Hill Station

I see you every day
Walk barefoot on the frozen ground.
I want to be your friend,
But you look the other way.

I see you every day
Go hungry in the bitter cold;
I'd gladly share my food,
But you look the other way.

I hear you every night
Cough desolately in the dark;
I'd share my warmth with you,
But you look the other way.

I see you every day
Pass lonely on my lonely way.
I'd gladly walk with you;
But you turn away.

Song of the Cockroach

We are the survivors,
Crow and I,
And beetle and bed-bug and bluebottle-fly.
We dine on your refuse,
Exult in your drains,
Your poisons can't touch us—
You'll not hear us complain.
When you choke on your gases
And drown in their fumes,
All the rot in your gutters
Are the choicest perfumes.
So carry on turning
Earth's treasures to ruins,
We will sit here and laugh
While you build your own tombs.

Self-Portrait

There was an old man in Landour
Who wanted young folk to laugh more;
So he wrote them a book,
And with laughter they shook
As they rolled down the hill to Rajpore.

Haikus

Whenever I am in a pensive or troubled state, I read (or write) a Haiku. It helps to clear and calm my mind. Here are a few that I wrote last year…

> Sweet-scented jasmine in this fold of cloth
> I give to you on this your bridal day,
> That you forget me not.

*

> There's a begonia in her cheeks,
> Pink as the flush of early dawn
> On Sikkim's peaks.

*

> Her beauty brought her fame.
> But only the wild rose flowering beside her grave
> Is there to hear her whispered name.

*

> Bright red
> The poinsettia flames
> As autumn and the old year wanes.

*

Red geranium
Gleaming against the rain-bright floor…
Memory, hold the door!

*

The Indian Pink keeps flowering without end,
Sturdy and modest,
A loyal friend.

*

Shaded in a deep ravine,
The ferns stand upright,
Dark and green.

*

When I was a boy, I dreamt of
wealth and fame;
And now I'm old, I dream of being
a boy again.

*

Jasmine flowers in her hair,
Languid summer days are here,
And sweet longing scents the air.

*

One fine day my kite took wing,
Then came a strong wind—
I was left with the string!

*

To the temple on the mountain top
We climbed. Forgot to pray!
But got home anyway.

*

Portents

The spiders on my bedroom wall gave rise to the following lines:

> This little spider,
> His name is Paul;
> He loves to crawl all over my wall.
>
> This little spider,
> His name is Bhim;
> His legs are quite long,
> But he doesn't swim.
>
> Here's a third spider,
> Her name is Sue;
> And if she gets hungry,
> She'll eat those two!
>
> Spider running up the wall
> Means that rain is going to fall.
>
> Spider running down the wall
> Means the house is going to fall!

Good Omens, Good Companions

Pigeons cooing on the roof. A calming effect.

*

The little skink living beneath a flower-pot.
Do not disturb.

*

The stray dog who sleeps on my steps
whenever fireworks are being let off in the street.
Only humans like loud noises.

*

The wild cat that crawls into the space
between the rafters and the roof late at night.
    I seldom see him, but
    I know he's there and he knows
I'm here.

Consolations

1

At night, the rain drumming on the corrugated
> tin roof.

And, early in the morning, when the rain
> has stopped:

A crow shaking the raindrops from his feathers.
The sweet ascending trill of a whistling thrush.
Dogs rushing through the damp undergrowth.
A great wild dahlia, its scarlet flowers drenched
> and heavy.

2

A mountain stream, always in a hurry, bubbling
> over rocks and

chattering, 'I'm late, I'm late!' like the
> White Rabbit,

tumbling over itself in its anxiety to reach the
> bottom of the hill.

3

The sound of the sea, especially when it's
> far away—

or when you hear it in the seashell you put to
 your ear.

4

After a long dry spell, raindrops on a dusty road
and after a summer shower,
raindrops on a sunflower.

To Light a Fire

To light a fire
We must kneel.
To change a tyre,
We must descend;
To pluck a flower,
We bend;
To lift a child,
We bend again;
To touch an elder's feet
We do the same.
For prayer, or play, or just plain mending,
There's something to be said for bending!

Night in the Mountains: Garhwal

A buffalo herd winding its way homewards in the twilight. Mist trailing up the valleys, and the hill thick with ferns and wild flowers. The gurgle of hookahs and the smell of cow-dung smoke. On the hill across the valley, lights begin to flicker—the dim light of kerosene lamps swing in the dark.

I stretch myself out on the charpai under a short, squat lime tree, and a sky tremendous with stars. The moon has not yet risen and the cicadas are silent. As I close my eyes, someone brushes against the lime tree, bruising its leaves, and the good fresh fragrance of lime comes to me on the night air.

Night in the Hills: Landour

Darkness falls, and it is time to pull my chair to the window. Much that is lovely comes at this hour.

There is the fragrance of raat ki rani, queen of the night, from a neighbour's balcony, two feet by two. And soon there will be the moonlight falling on those white flowers, and a moonbeam in my room. Sometimes a field mouse drops in for a bite (he remembers my dinnertime). High in the treetops, an owl hoots softly, as if testing, trying to remember. The nightjar plays trombone, and the crickets join in to complete the orchestra. They go silent when the swamp deer calls. A leopard is out hunting.

A breeze has sprung up, it hums in the trees, and now the window is rattling. Time to shut the window. A star falls in the heavens.

Out of the Dark

At a ruin upon a hill outside the town,
I found some shelter from a summer storm.
An alcove in a wall, moss-green and redolent
    of bats
But refuge from the wind and rain; and
    entrance once
To what had been a home, a mansion large
    and spacious;
Now dream-wrecked, desolate.
And as I stood there, pondering
Upon the mutability of stone, I thought I heard
A haunting cry, insistent on the wind—
'Oh son, please let me in,
Oh son, please let me in…'

Just the soughing of the wind
In the bending, keening pines;
Just the rain sibilant on old stones;
Or was it something more, a voice
Trapped in the woof of time, imploring still,
And lingering at some door which stood
When now I sheltered on a barren hill.

At home, that night, I settled down
To read, the bedlamp on. The night was warm,
The storm had passed, and all was still outside,
When something, someone, moved about, came
    tapping on the door.
'Who's there?' I called.
The tapping stopped. And then,
Entreating, came that voice again:
'Oh son, please let me in!'
'Who's there, who's there?' I cried,
And crossed the cold, stone floor,
Paused for a moment, hand on catch,
Then opened wide the door.
Bright moonlight streamed across the sill,
And crept along the stair;
I peered outside, to right and left:
Bright road returned my stare.

But long before the dawn, I heard
That tapping once again;
Not on the door this time, but nearer still—
Now rapping quickly on the window-pane.
I lay quite still and held my breath
And thought—surely it's the old oak tree,
Leaves gently tapping on the glass,
Or a moth, or some great beetle winging past.
But through the darkness, pressing in,
As though in me it sought its will,
As though in me it yet would dwell,

Odds and Ends / 173

'Oh son, please let me in…
Oh son, please let me in!'

All Is Life

Whether by accident or design,
We are here.
Let's make the most of it, my friend.
Make happiness our pursuit,
Spread a little sunshine here and there.
Enjoy the flowers, the breeze,
Rivers, sea, and sky,
Mountains and tall waving trees.
Greet the children passing by,
Talk to the old folk.
Be kind, my friend.
Hold on, in times of pain and strife:
Until death comes, all is life.

At the Grave of John Mildenhall in Agra

In the year 1594,
Visiting first Lahore
And then the garden city of Ajmer,
Came a merchant adventurer,
John Mildenhall by name,
From London by the River Thame.
To Agra's mart he brought
His goods and baggage; then sought
Audience with the great
Moghul, who sat in state
In a vast red sandstone audience-hall.
'We are pleased, Mr Mildenhall,
To have you at our court,' great Akbar said;
'Your Queen is known to have an astute head,
Your country many ships, and I hear
Of a poet called Shakespeare—
Who, though not as good as Fazl or Faiz,
Writes a pretty line and does plays on the side.
But tell us—when will you be on your way?'
'Most gracious King, I'd like to stay—
With your permission—for a while',
Said the traveller with the Elizabethan smile.

To this request the Emperor complied.
John stayed, and settled down, and died.
Over three hundred years had passed
When those who followed, left at last.

Last Words

Observing Ananda weeping, Gautama said,
'O Ananda do not weep. This body of ours
contains within itself the powers which renew
its strength for a time, but also the causes which
lead to its destruction. Is there anything put
together which shall not dissolve?'
Then, turning to his disciples, he said, 'When
I am passed away and am no longer with you,
do not think the Buddha has left you, and is not
still in your midst. You have my words, my
explanations, my laws…' And again, 'Beloved
disciples, if you love my memory, love one another.'
And after another pause he said, 'Beloved,
that which causes life causes also decay
and death. Never forget this. I called you to tell
    you this.'
These were the last words of Gautama
Buddha, as he stretched himself out and died
under the great sal tree, at Kasinagara.

Hold on to Your Dreams

Hold on to your dreams,
    and don't let go!
Follow the rainbow,
The tide in its flow,
Salute the sun
    at the break of day
Find time for the flowers
    along the way
Follow the birds
    as they come and go.
Hold on to your dreams
    and don't let go!

Dare to Dream

Build castles in the air
But first, give them foundations.
Hold fast to all your dreams,
Make perfect your creations.
All glory comes to those who dare.
Failed works are sad lame things.
Act impeccably, sing
Your own song, but do not take
Another's song from her or him;
Look for your art within,
You'll find your own true gift,
For you are special too.
And if you try, you'll find
There's nothing you can't do.

We Who Love Books

Some books I'll never give away,
Though old and worn, their binding torn,
Upon my shelves they'll always stay,
Alive, still read, still fresh each dawn,
Their magic moments never gone.

Great verse, great thoughts, still stand the test
Of time that's passing by so fast…
These good companions never fail
To give us joy, to nourish us…
We who love books will always be
The lucky ones,
Our minds set free.

These Simple Things

The simplest things in life are best—
A patch of green,
A small bird's nest,
A drink of water, fresh and cold,
The taste of bread,
A song of old,
These are the things that matter most.
The laughter of a child,
A favourite book,
Flowers growing wild,
A cricket singing in a shady nook,
A ball that bounces high!
A summer shower,
A rainbow in the sky,
The touch of a loving hand,
And time to rest—
These simple things in life are best.

And As We Part

The day is done,
It's time to sleep,
And with this world
To make my peace.
Enchanted days
Have all my life
Brought beauty
More than bitter strife.
May you who read
These words today
Be blessed in every way…
And as we part,
I give you all
That lies within my heart.

Ruskin Bond

Ruskin Bond has written novels, memoirs, short story collections and books of essays and poetry. His recent books include *Lone Fox Dancing: My Autobiography*, *A Book of Simple Living: Brief Notes from the HIlls*, *Friends in Wild Places: Birds, Beasts and Other Companions*, *A Little Book of Happiness*, *A Little Book of Serenity* and *A Little Book of Love and Companionship*, as well as the popular classics *Room on the Roof* (winner of the John Llewellyn Rhys Prize), *A Flight of Pigeons*, *The Blue Umbrella*, *Time Stops at Shamli*, *Night Train at Deoli*, *Our Trees Still Grow in Dehra* (winner of the Sahitya Akademi Award) and *Rain in the Mountains*. He has co-edited *Himalaya: Adventures, Meditations, Life* (with Namita Gokhale) and *Prankenstein: The Book of Crazy Mischief* (with Jerry Pinto). He was awarded the Padma Shri by the Government of India in 1999 and the Padma Bhushan in 2014.

www.ingramcontent.com/pod-product-compliance
Lightning Source LLC
Chambersburg PA
CBHW061940220426
43662CB00012B/1973